Super Mario Party

Beginner's Guide

T0061949

21st Century Skills **INNOVATION LIBRARY**

Josh Gregory

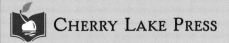

Published in the United States of America by Cherry Lake Publishing Group
Ann Arbor, Michigan
www.cherrylakepublishing.com

Reading Adviser: Beth Walker Gambro, MS, Ed., Reading Consultant, Yorkville, IL

Photo Credits: ©LightField Studios / Shutterstock, 5; ©Vantage_DS / Shutterstock, 8

Cherry Lake Press is an imprint of Cherry Lake Publishing Group.

Library of Congress Cataloging-in-Publication Data has been filed and is available at catalog.loc.gov

Cherry Lake Publishing Group would like to acknowledge the work of the Partnership for 21st Century Learning, a Network of Battelle for Kids. Please visit http://www.battelleforkids.org/networks/p21 for more information.

Printed in the United States of America
Corporate Graphics

Josh Gregory is the author of more than 125 books for kids. He has written about everything from animals to technology to history. A graduate of the University of Missouri–Columbia, he currently lives in Chicago, Illinois.

Contents

CHAPTER 1

Party Hard

Throughout history, people have always enjoyed getting together to hold friendly competitions. And for thousands of years, board games have been among the most popular ways to play. Games like chess, go, and backgammon have stood the test of time for centuries. These classic board games are designed so well that they have stayed more or less exactly the same since they were created, and people today enjoy them just as much as their ancestors did.

At the same time, games are always evolving and changing. People design new games and new types of games. In recent decades, one of the biggest developments has come in the form of video games. And from the very beginning of video game history, board games were a big influence on **developers**. Back in the 1960s and 1970s, when video games were still a very new form of technology, many computer programmers worked hard to create computers capable of playing games like chess against human opponents. And since then, countless popular board games have been turned into video games, from Monopoly to Risk. These virtual versions of classic games solve some of the drawbacks of real board games: They don't take much time to set up and get started, and there are no small pieces that can get lost. However, they aren't that different from playing the original version of the game.

Traditional board games like Monopoly are usually most fun to play the old-fashioned way.

A Natural Fit

Believe it or not, Nintendo was founded more than 130 years ago. Of course, the company did not make video games at first. It began in 1889 as a manufacturer of Japanese playing cards called *hanafuda*. Over time, the company expanded and started making a variety of toys. Among them were board games. As Nintendo became famous for video games in the 1980s, it stopped selling these other products. But in some ways, the *Mario Party* series is just Nintendo getting back to what it's always done best: creating fun games for people to enjoy together, whether they are video games, board games, or something in between.

In 1998, video game giant Nintendo released a new game called *Mario Party* for the Nintendo 64 console. *Mario Party* was a video board game unlike anything that had come before. It featured all the standard parts of a traditional board game along with Nintendo's most famous characters and settings. Players rolled virtual dice and moved their pieces around a virtual board. But *Mario Party* also offered something that no board game could: the fast-paced action gameplay of a traditional video game.

As *Mario Party* players move around a virtual board, they must also occasionally compete in a variety of minigames. These minigames can be anything from racing or bowling to memory contests or mazes. Some pit all the players in the game against each other. Others are team efforts. Each minigame takes just a couple of minutes or less. Performing well in them is essential to success in *Mario Party*. No matter how lucky you get with your dice rolls, it's tough to win without doing well in the minigames.

Mario Party's combination of classic board games with modern-day video game action was an immediate

Many minigames ask players to use game controllers in unique ways. In this one, players must use a combination of buttons and motion controls to act like they are gripping and climbing a pole.

success. It has spawned more than a dozen sequels and spinoffs and sold tens of millions of copies. Each new entry in the series features dozens of new minigames, new game boards to play on, and sometimes other twists to help keep the classic formula fresh. Countless players around the world have grown up playing the games with their friends and family, and today the *Mario Party* series is just as beloved as any traditional physical board game.

In *Super Mario Party,* each player will use a single Joy-Con controller, rather than a pair.

In October 2018, *Super Mario Party* was released for the Nintendo Switch. It was designed to be the perfect entry point to the series for new players. Thanks to the wild success of the Switch and the enduring popularity of the *Mario Party* series, it has proved to be a massive hit.

Whether you're a longtime *Mario Party* master or you've never played before, you never know when you might find yourself in the middle of an intense *Super Mario Party* competition with friends. When that happens, you'll want to be prepared. With dozens of minigames and plenty of potential winning strategies, there's a lot to learn.

CHAPTER 2

The First Game

When you first fire up *Super Mario Party*, you'll find yourself walking around an area called the Party Plaza. You can walk and jump and talk to the characters hanging around the plaza. But even though you are controlling a character, this area is basically just the main menu of the game. Here, you can choose how many human players will join and which characters they will play as. You can also choose which game mode you want to play. To make your selection, simply walk up to one of the big video screens and press the A button.

Several game modes are available to play right from the start. The main mode you will probably find yourself using the most is simple called Mario Party mode. This is the classic board game where four players will take turns rolling dice and moving around a board as they try to earn coins and stars. If you don't have four human players, you can also add computer-controlled players to fill up a game.

Partner Party mode is very similar to Mario Party mode. The main difference is that you will play as two teams of two players each. To succeed, you'll need to cooperate and plan out your moves with your teammate.

River Survival is very different. In this mode, you'll find yourself in a raft with three other players. All four

Each player's movements have an effect on the direction of the raft in River Survival.

players need to hold their controllers like oars and move them to paddle down a river. As the raft moves down the river, a timer will count down. You can steer the raft toward little clocks to gain more time. You can also pop balloons to start minigames. Doing well in a minigame will also add time to the clock. At branches in the river, you can choose which way to go. Each path has different obstacles that can make it hard to steer. Players will need to cooperate the whole time to make it to the end of the course before the timer runs out.

It takes careful timing and a good sense of rhythm to succeed at Sound Stage mode.

Sound Stage is another mode that doesn't have much to do with board games. In this one, all four players will compete in a series of events where they need to move and shake their controllers to the rhythm of the music. Moving your controller at the right moment will earn you coins, and the player with the most coins at the end is the winner.

Want to enjoy the minigames of *Super Mario Party* without committing to one of the longer modes? Simply visit the blue toad in front of the video screen

Online Competition

You don't need to get all your friends together in the same room to enjoy *Super Mario Party* together. The Mario Party, Partner Party, and Minigames modes all offer the option for online play. This wasn't always the case, though. When the game was first released, there was no option to play the main Mario Party and Partner Party modes online. Players could only challenge each other to Minigames. Many reviewers and players were unhappy about this missing feature. But more than 2 years after the game's release, in April 2021, Nintendo released a new patch that improved the game's online options. It came as a huge surprise, but a very welcome one.

marked Minigames. Here, you can practice any of the minigames you have played so far in the main modes. There are also a couple of options for competing against other players in a series of minigames, and you can even check a list of records showing your best attempts at all the different minigames. This mode is a great way to practice if minigames aren't your strongest suit.

The main board game modes are definitely the main attraction in *Super Mario Party*. The first step in any

Minigames mode lets you sample some fun parts of *Super Mario Party* without committing to a full game.

match is to choose which board you want to play on. There are three of them available to start with, and each one has a different theme and different obstacles and gimmicks. Whomp's Domino Ruins has a jungle setting. King Bob-omb's Powderkeg Mine is full of burning hot lava. Megafruit Paradise gives you the chance to enjoy an island adventure.

Once you choose a board, you can decide how many turns you want the game to last: 10, 15, or 20. More turns leads to a longer, more competitive game. But even the shortest game will take about an hour. You can always save progress and pick up a game where you left off, but it is usually more fun to get through a whole game in one sitting.

At the start of each game, the four players roll dice to determine the order they will move in throughout the game. This detail will have a huge effect on how the game plays out, especially near the end. But the order will not give anyone a built-in advantage.

When it's your turn, you get to choose whether to roll the normal six-sided dice or your character's special dice block. Each character's special block is different. Some might offer a blend of very high and very low numbers. Others might have similar numbers on almost every side, making it easier to predict how many spaces you will get to move.

As you move around the board, you want to try and reach stars before other players. Stars are the most

Always try to get as many stars as you can in Mario Party mode. It's the only way to win!

You'll get coins from landing on certain spaces, doing well in minigames, and more.

important thing in the game. The player with the most stars at the end of the final turn is the winner. There is always a single star on the board at any given time. Its location will change throughout the game depending on what happens, so you can't always predict where you need to go. You have to think quickly and be willing to change plans when you need to.

You will also earn coins as you move around the board. These are useful for all kinds of reasons. You can use them to buy items if you land near a shop. You can also trade them for stars when you reach the right spots on the board. Try to collect as many as you can.

At the end of each turn, after each player has rolled the dice and moved, it's time for a minigame. Which minigame you play is random. Some of them are team-based, while in others each player is on their own. Before the minigame starts, you will see a short

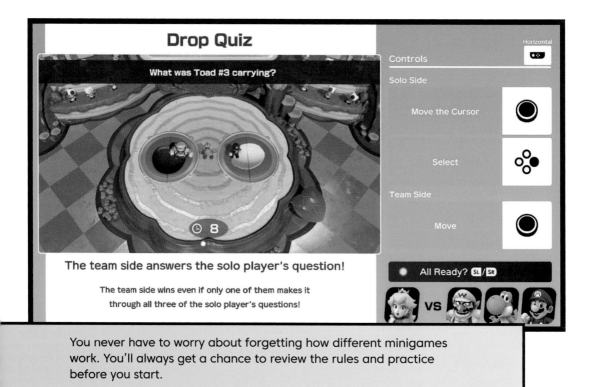

You never have to worry about forgetting how different minigames work. You'll always get a chance to review the rules and practice before you start.

explanation and get a chance to practice, so don't worry if it's your first time.

You should also keep a close eye out for ally spaces as you play. If you land on one, you can gain an ally to move around alongside you. This ally will have their own dice that add to your roll. You can pick up several allies over the course of a game if you're lucky. The more you have, the better your odds of winning will be.

Simply keep rolling the dice and thinking strategically to collect coins and stars. At the end of the final turn, you will find out who the winner is. It might sound simple, but there is a lot of skill and strategy involved.

CHAPTER 3

Roll of the Dice

Super Mario Party will give you plenty to do right from the start. However, there are even more things you can unlock as you play, from new characters and boards to entire game modes.

As soon as you have played at least one round of Mario Party mode, go to the Party Plaza and head to the right. You will see a green pipe that was previously blocked off. Jump inside to get access to Toad's Rec Room. This mode lets you play a variety of special minigames. For example, there is a baseball game where players can pitch the ball and swing the bat using motion controls. Some of the Toad's Rec Room minigames even allow you to hook up more than one Switch system to play games that would be impossible on a single screen.

Another unlockable mode is called Challenge Road. This mode opens up after you have played every minigame in the other modes at least once. There are 80 of them, and they are spread across Mario Party, Partner Party, River Survival, and Sound Stage modes. Challenge Road is a single player mode where you face a long string of minigames and are asked to meet a variety of special challenges. It's meant for players who have already gotten very good at the minigames, so it can be pretty tough.

One of the games in Toad's Rec Room lets you play motion-controlled baseball against a friend.

There are 4 secret characters you can unlock in *Super Mario Party*, in addition to the 16 characters available from the start. Like any of the other characters, each of the hidden ones has a unique dice block that can really change how you play the game.

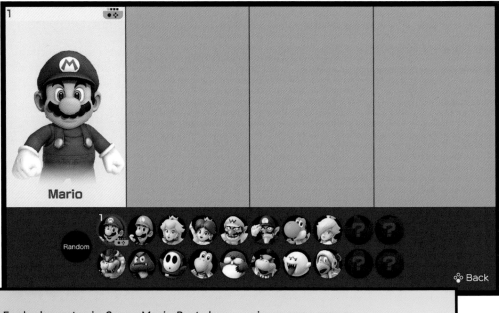

Each character in *Super Mario Party* has a unique appearance, personality, and play style.

Bowser

You're smarter than you look!
Let's do this.

It's worth talking to everyone you meet in the Party Plaza to see what happens.

The simplest character to unlock is Dry Bones, the skeleton Koopa Troopa. Simply keep playing the game, trying new modes, and completing matches. At some point, you will find him hanging out in the Party Plaza. Talk to him and he will be added to your character list. He shows up at random times, so there is no specific way to make him appear.

If you want to unlock the legendary Donkey Kong, you'll need to spend some time playing River Survival mode. Finish three different paths down the river and then return to the Party Plaza to find him waiting.

The last two characters can be unlocked by playing Challenge Road mode. Donkey Kong's sidekick Diddy Kong will arrive in the Party Plaza after you complete world two of Challenge Road, while Pom Pom makes her appearance after you finish world five.

What's Next?

Nintendo seems to always be working on the next *Mario Party*, so it's rarely a huge surprise when a new title gets announced. The main thing fans get excited about is seeing what kind of spin each new game will put on the classic formula.

In Summer of 2021, Nintendo announced that the follow-up to *Super Mario Party* would be called *Mario Party Superstars*. The twist this time is simple: The new game will bring back classic minigames and boards from *Mario Party* games of the past, but with the modern graphics and other improvements seen in *Super Mario Party*. For longtime fans, it will be a chance to revisit the reasons they fell in love with the series. And newcomers will get a chance to experience the best the series has to offer.

Want to play on a new game board? All you need to do is play on each of the starting boards at least once. This will open up the option to play Mario Party and Partner Party modes in Kamek's Tantalizing Tower, a sparkling tower that seems to be made of solid gold.

Another thing you can work to unlock are the five hidden gems. Finding these gems is your main goal if you are interested in seeing the storyline of *Super Mario Party*. Each one is hidden behind one of the game's main modes. The Gem of **Tenacity** is unlocked after you have played all four boards in Mario Party mode, while the Gem of Love comes from playing those boards in Partner Party mode. You'll earn the Gem of Spirit when you finish the hardest difficulty of Sound Stage mode, and the Gem of Courage unlocks after you have finished every path down the river in River Survival mode. Finally, you can get the Gem of Passion by finishing every world in Challenge Road. Once you have them all, you'll see a special scene. By that point, you'll also be a pro at *Super Mario Party*!

CHAPTER 4

Improving Your Odds

There's no getting around it: It takes some good luck and favorable rolls of the dice to succeed in *Super Mario Party*. Things aren't always going to go your way, no matter how well you play. However, the game is not entirely based on luck. There are all kinds of strategies you can use to give yourself the edge over your opponents.

One thing that will definitely give you an advantage is learning the ins and outs of each of the game's boards. Each of them is arranged differently, and there are all kinds of special features on each one that aren't on the others. For example, there are often warp pipes that let you zip from one part of the board to another, or special spaces that can be used to alter the landscape and mess up your opponents' plans. Knowing how to make your way to different points on the board as quickly as possible is key. As new stars pop up or shift locations, you can be the first to reach them.

Similarly, practicing minigames will always give you an edge. Better performance in minigames leads to more coins. This gives you more opportunities to buy items and stars. One of the worst situations is when you get

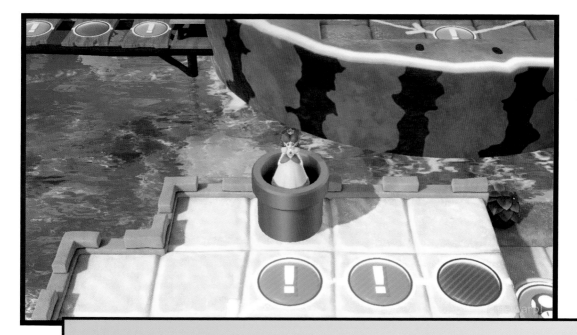

Landing at a warp pipe at just the right time can put you much closer to snagging a star.

to a star before anyone else and you don't have any coins. You have to give up your opportunity to buy the star!

Items can really turn the tide if you use them carefully. Sometimes you will get opportunities to buy them as you move around the board. You can hold up to four of

Knowing that you have the option to add a certain number to your rolls can really change your dice-rolling strategy.

Buy items whenever you can, but try to make sure you always save some coins for stars.

them at a time, but you can only use one per turn. Items do everything from adding numbers to your dice rolls to stealing coins from opponents or warping you across the board. Resist the temptation to use them as soon as you get them. Instead, let your opponents forget that you are packing a powerful item, and then deploy it when it is most effective and they least expect it. Don't wait too long to use your items though. Especially in the last few turns, it's good to use your items up so they won't go to waste.

Think carefully about where you want to move before rolling the dice. Then choose the right dice block to help you meet that goal. For example, your character's special block might focus on the middle numbers, like threes and fours. But if you need to get farther than that, it might be better to take a gamble with the regular dice block. And if you're packing an item to add three to your roll, it might be a no-brainer. No matter what, there will always be a risk that your roll won't get you where you need to be. The trick is to try and make sure the odds are greater that you will reach your target than not.

Friends and Rivals

As you make your way across the board, you might find situations where you and another player could help each other. For example, perhaps one player has taken a huge lead over the other three. It makes sense for the players who are lagging behind to team up against the lead player whenever possible to try and even the odds. Remember that Mario Party mode isn't a team game, though. A player might do something that helps you out on one turn, only to cause big problems for you on the next. Work together when it is useful, but always look out for number one!

Mario suggested having a party to decide, a time-honored tradition.

S1 / S2 Skip

Like Mario says, it's always a good idea to have a party with friends!

No matter what, you won't win every time you play. But it's not always about winning. *Super Mario Party* is all about getting together with friends to have a good time. The important part is right there in the game's title: it's a party game. So get some people together, break out the snacks, and throw a board game bash!

GLOSSARY

developers (dih-VEL-uh-purz) people who make video games or other computer programs

patch (PATCH) an update to a game or other computer program that is created after the program is released

tenacity (teh-NA-sih-tee) the ability to stick to something, even when it is difficult

FIND OUT MORE

Books

Cunningham, Kevin. *Video Game Designer*. Ann Arbor, MI: Cherry Lake Publishing, 2016.

Loh-Hagan, Virginia. *Video Games*. Ann Arbor, MI: Cherry Lake Publishing, 2021.

Powell, Marie. *Asking Questions About Video Games*. Ann Arbor, MI: Cherry Lake Publishing, 2016.

Websites

Super Mario Party for Nintendo Switch
www.nintendo.com/games/detail/super-mario-party-switch/
Watch some videos and learn more about the different features of *Super Mario Party*.

Mario Party Superstars for Nintendo Switch
www.nintendo.com/games/detail/mario-party-superstars-switch/
Check out the latest updates on the upcoming sequel to *Super Mario Party*.

INDEX